Space: Is That Really Empty?

Austin John N. Arnaiz

Ukiyoto Publishing

All global publishing rights are held by

Ukiyoto Publishing

Published in 2024

Content Copyright © Austin John N. Arnaiz

ISBN 9789362695581

All rights reserved.

No part of this publication may be reproduced, transmitted, or stored in a retrieval system, in any form by any means, electronic, mechanical, photocopying, recording or otherwise, without the prior permission of the publisher.

The moral rights of the author have been asserted.

This is a work of fiction. Names, characters, businesses, places, events, locales, and incidents are either the products of the author's imagination or used in a fictitious manner. Any resemblance to actual persons, living or dead, or actual events is purely coincidental.

This book is sold subject to the condition that it shall not by way of trade or otherwise, be lent, resold, hired out or otherwise circulated, without the publisher's prior consent, in any form of binding or cover other than that in which it is published.

www.ukiyoto.com

Dedication

It was January 08, 2022 that the author of this book after publishing his recently manuscript about his understanding on the science of electricity, was struck by another idea, the idea that barely no one wishes to write and explain. As humans were so busy living their daily routine that we don't have the time to ask every simple yet complicated questions of our curious minds. Let's just don't take everything for granted in this world. Life is short, so anyone who grasped the opportunity to learn or even visualized the designs of the workings of nature sometime in his life is intellectual to anyone. Ask questions out of your curious mind like a child holding the alphabet blocks, like the eyes observing the butterflies...

Like the title of my second book, "What is Really Going on With That Electric Spark?", I want to continue my writing journey on things that our mind barely questions. "Space: Is That Really Empty?", the words came out of my mind as I reminisced my childhood's curious mind. For sure, everyone would say, "of course! space is empty, that's why we can move and perform mobility on space because there are nothing occupying it, hence, it's "empty". It is a no-brainer question for a typical reader but will tickle the imagination of someone interested on understanding the science behind it.

This short informative manuscript would not continue without the guidance and knowledge from the Lord. He gave me the drive, creativity and ideas to pursue the concepts and visualizations for the readers that I want to present. I am overwhelmed that God had given me this third chance to publish another book, and from this, I am sincerely thanking Him.

For those who are in doubts if I really wrote the content of this book myself or being guided by an artificial intelligence, I will let you check it by the help of an AI checker in the internet and it's free! Or in any case that there might be phrases similar to the works of an AI, the author is certainly believing that the content of this book is not mostly made or mostly guided by artificial intelligence.

In addition, the proofs that it is most likely human-written were included in the last pages.

This third book will not be the last miniature of mine. I will keep writing my passion, as the interest of many inspires me to author several more. Thanks be to God! He is the sole author of everything.

"As we are mortals having a limited time in this world, build things in which are immortal and cannot be forgotten, build your legacy."

Austin John N. Arnaiz

Contents

Prologue	1
Introduction	2
Chapter 1-The Minute Universes	10
Chapter 2-The Bizarre World of Sub-atomics	24
Chapter 3-Within a Blue Planet	31
Chapter 4-The Vastness of the Realm of Space	40
Chapter 5-The World of Multiverses	47
Glossary of Terms	56
About the Author	61
Proofs that the Book is Most Likely Human Written	62

Prologue

I certainly believed that stormy weather really makes introverts comfortable. It was a Saturday morning and my eyes were so asleep that I could barely open them despite of hearing the swirling of leaves with the wind outside. I could not even try to sneak what is happening on my window. The weather is so cold that I could not let to move any of my arms. My blanket and my only pillow were the only thing that covered me from the coldness that morning. That was another stormy day and the sun is missing. As my mind could not even try to think the moment, my unconscious eyes closed again then I fell asleep and my mind placed me on worlds that I rarely see...

Introduction

Before you begin to tackle numerous pages about this book, I want to ask you a simple question, what comes into your mind when you heard the word "space"? Do you only think of stars, galaxies, and another realm outside of our planet? Is the space simply pertaining to the dark, vast worlds out there among the stars? What was "space" mean to you?

I certainly guess that the word "space" first comes to our vocabulary when we were a kid. When we were in awe just by looking at the shooting stars in the midnight sky. When we were looking in wonder at the moon above our eyes, that seemed to follow us wherever we go. The twinkling of the stars and the darkness of the sightings above, all were part of our understanding about the matters of space. I remember the time of my childhood that the news announced that after a few days, the image of Mars will be seen closely in the night sky. All were astounded by the information. We, together with my colleagues, waited for that time to come.

The said night finally arrived, and we rushed outside looking for the shiniest thing in the sky. We noticed the luminous sphere-like dot and looked in wonder at the clear view of the Martian's surface. It's like a party ball hanged high above the ceiling of the sky that it reflects some light shining our vivid eyes, a rare event that is unforgettable.

Since the time of intellectual capability, humans were asking themselves while looking at the sky at night, "Are there other living creatures up there looking at us?". "Are there other beings up there who live in a different world than I?". "What are their worlds look like?". "Are they conscious?". "How can they live their life to survive?" Those questions seem exciting to talk about.

The universe had left humans to wander in their imaginations, out of curiosity, the vastness of the fabric of space. The bright stars and the blazing suns, the beautiful auroras, fiery comets, and the dark, cold boulders silently roaming their orbit, the universe had plenty of entities to offer. It is due to the fact that there were hundreds of planets discovered residing the Milky Way Galaxy. In addition to the various forms of stars and heavenly bodies, our place in this vastness appears to be a grain of sand in a wide coastland, we are just unnoticeable.

The wide universe outside of outer space seemed to be an illogical setting for the average blue planet. I mean, what is the purpose of such existence? If human can barely set foot on the moon and still had difficulties travelling to Mars, plus the fact that the space in the universe is ever increasing through time, why is there a creation of such endless space?

It might be good considering that the space is not just the stage of our mobility and the existential place of our existence. Space is itself the medium of the senses to perform and function. We could not experience our vision if there is no space, as there are no medium for light to travel from the object to our eyes to see. Our hearing ability will be useless as sound needs space to travel. We could not smell at the first place if there is no space for the fragrance to move into. Our senses need space to perform its functionality.

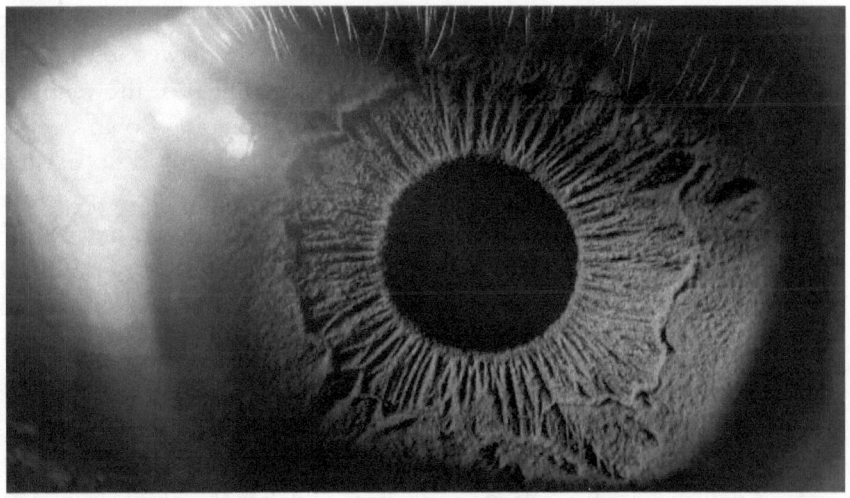

Figure 1. Remember that our eyes can only see about 380 to 700 nanometers of wavelength of light. There are numerous sightings hidden out there!

From the immeasurable darkness outside of Earth, humans knew that there are worlds out there, also wide enough to unravel and understand. That universe is roaming around, occupies our space, and existing within us: the vast emptiness of sub-atomic worlds. Atoms are almost empty spaces glued to each other to form elements, to form compounds, and to form any matter visible or invincible before our eyes. Particles residing the inside of each atom were so small that they only accounts to almost a minute percentage against its overall volume. All matter including us are just composed of spherical spaces with minute tangible objects in the center bunch and glued together in a systematical way to exist or coexist in nature.

> All matter including us are just composed of spherical spaces with minute tangible objects in the center bunch and glued together in a systematical way to exist or coexist in nature.

From the deepness of the sub-atomic worlds up to the vastness of the universe, humans left with plenty of questions to answer the reason and purpose of our existence. We are just in the midst of the vastness of the fabric of space, ever increasing in size and going down deeper and deeper through time. There are long old ages of time existed before us and endless history waiting for us in the future. Are those immeasurable distant past and future built and laid down before us? Or just the product of probabilities of histories? Surely, we could not talk about it as our senses were limited, in a minute scale compare to the vastness of information laying before our minds.

Humans were rational, we provide solutions to everyday problems, we are programmed to organize things to prepare for the better future. From that, it is not surprising to think that scientific notions about the laws of nature were leading to unification, which is the ultimate goal of science endeavors. From every single discovery inside the laboratory, the propositions explaining each phenomenon, and theories

contributing to the truthfulness of the workings of nature, were leading to a single pathway of choice: the single ultimate law of the universe. Henceforth, physicists are trying to unify laws from different arenas, especially the laws combining the science of sub-atomic worlds and the wideness of the universe. This then later called the Theory of Everything. Mr. Albert Einstein, who passionately tried to combine the two, for 30 years, didn't succeed until the year of his death.

In the present time, science is almost unified, except on the two colossal fields of the latter worlds. But at least, in each world was governed by a specified number of laws unified to explain each scientific event in general sense. General sense means, what is happening nearby, could happen anywhere in the universe. These laws of nature could predict the event in future time, or visualize what happened in the past. Humans were gifted to understand the laws of nature despite of our senses' limitations.

> Humans were gifted to understand the laws of
> nature despite of our senses' limitations.

I am always wondering on the complexity and simplicity of the laws of nature. Since childhood, I am amazed to grasp the idea that the laws of science from here on Earth up to beyond the cosmos were all almost driven by the same arrays of principles. Wandering in your imagination, in different worlds and universes, that you may see the laws of Physics can be crafted from the same set of equations, discovered by our classical and modern scientists, used to describe everyday phenomena and have views in future predictions. Theoretical physicists are craving for answers where those laws originated. At the heart of the big bang, before the colossal explosion, are these laws predetermined or just the product of various probabilities of nature?

Through ages, my understanding of the laws of science gradually widened up until it cost me to believe that if multiverses exist, it may be governed with different scientific laws of science. That idea seems to open up various propositions and knowledge about our place in the history of time, if proven to be true. For now, one thing is for sure, the present laws of nature originated after some time from the Big Bang, where all elements and matter gradually existed.

Entities from within the inside of the center of an atom to the outside of our planet up to the entirety of heavenly abyss, were dominated and connected by one single entity of nature, the space. This entity is so predominant, that it houses all of universe's matter and even the

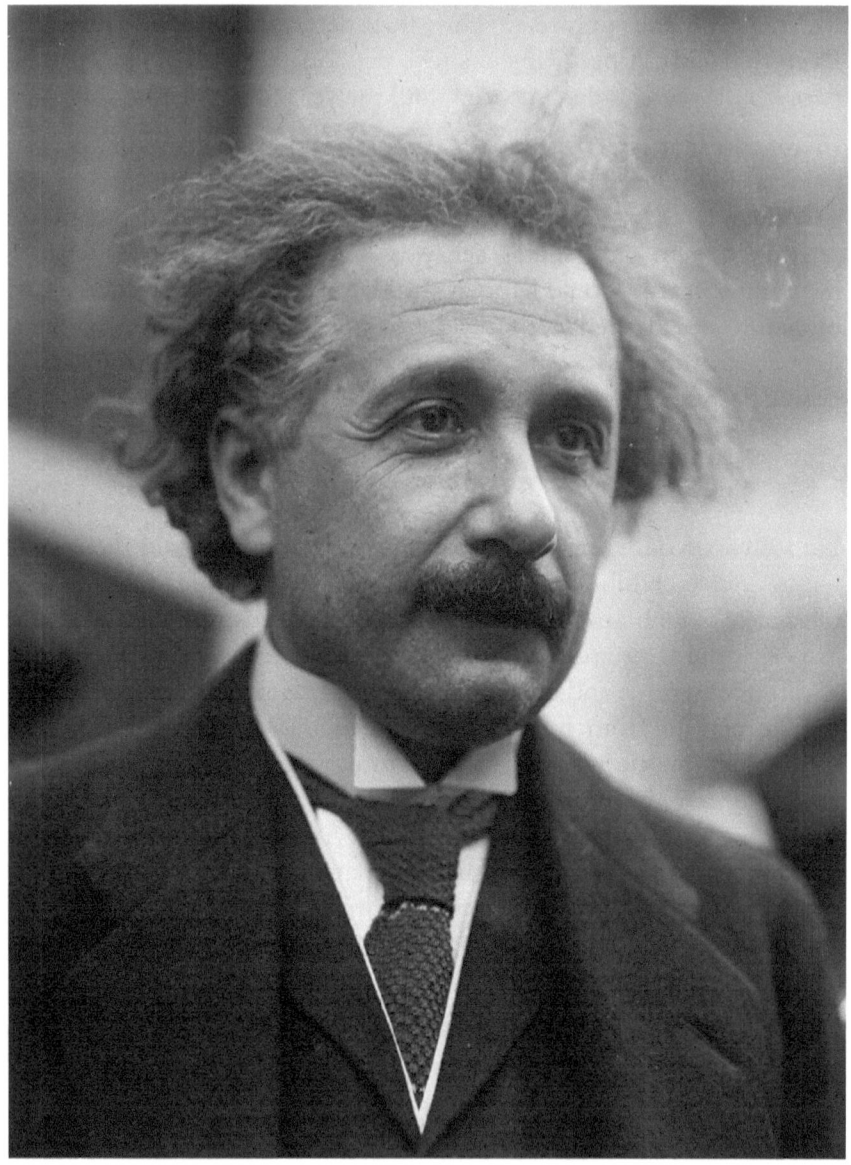

Figure 2. Albert Einstein, was a German-born theoretical physicist who is widely known as one of the greatest and most influential scientists of all time.

unknowns ever since the history of time. The space is where the laws are behaving, it is the stage of scientific immortality, the witness of everyday phenomena, the beholder of the true test of time.

Contrary to popular belief, every mortal used to think and accepted the fact that the word "space" is the emptiness in which matters are moving. I mean, what else could we think or imagine on an empty box where nothing resides and moves unless we put something in it? Space is the synonym for emptiness, that's what everybody knew. That proposition seemed to be in its final structure unless we think of it differently and in different perspective. Ready yourself before I tell you that the "space" you are thinking about is not empty, there is something in it that our eyes cannot see or detect by our instruments.

We must don't fool ourselves with our senses. Remember that we only see a tiny strands of wavelengths somewhat in the middle of the wide range of electromagnetic spectrum, those colors are in set of what we see at rainbows, ranging from reddish to greenish to violet kinds, each has different wavelengths as interpreted by our eyes. Each of the combinations of those colors are the product of what we see in the world around us. Those wavelengths are just riding in the fabric of space, using the space as the medium of propagation. Scientists ask a somewhat logical question, "If space itself is like a wave that ripples when subjected to "external" entities, what is the wave of space itself? The word "external" here means entities interact and affecting the behavior of the rippling of space, the best example is matter. If space ripples, there could be something in it that do the rippling. Something beyond human capability to observe and experiment. Something in which only human imagination can visualize, at least for now.

Think of black holes. They're just the super entity scattered in the wide void of our universe. Swallowing stars, asteroids and even light, like a monster starving for hunger, nothing could escape their immense gravitational pull. In fact, black holes are the center of every galaxy residing in the universe. What really are they? How can the largest entities be swallowed into nothingness and there are no traces left behind? (as perceived by our eyes) The scientific analogies of the structure and workings of a black hole serve a good representation of the real meaning of space. As stated earlier, space is not nothingness, it was a medium having "something" that human eyes and instruments can't really detect or feel its presence. Declaring it as a nothingness is an easier task. We knew that a black hole is created after the explosion of a dead star. After all the hundreds of years of continuous combustion, the particles that make up the stars will eventually be consumed itself and ripped apart. The aftermath is a point in space where the medium as the "space" itself is also consumed or destroyed by the explosion, hence, creating a hole. That "hole" doesn't do the rippling because there is literally no space entity that ripples. It is the true representation of the emptiness or nothingness. So, technically speaking, space is not empty, but if we are talking about the void of the center of the black hole, then you are correct, because black hole does have an empty "space".

The other way to clearly imagine the right representation of space is thinking that we are like the fishes in the sea. Look at them, they breath underwater, they live within the water bodies and can't live without it. The water itself is their space. Imagine that we were a fish and that we don't have any idea about the world outside, and all of a sudden, there was a sink hole on the ocean floor, swallowing all the corals and fishes nearby its mouth. The fishes can't barely resist to move away as their space, the water, is being swallowed too. They were carried by their spaces. The sink hole became the void in their environment. What really is that "hole?", and where do my fish friends landed on after getting swallowed? That scenario is like the black holes of our universe. It absorbs all the nearby stars and heavenly bodies even light, as light travels in space, and the space is getting swallowed too like the water by the sink hole.

> Through time, the philosophical thoughts were gradually replaced by scientific analogies.

If you were to tell me the greatest potential of man that prospered and remained successful throughout the ages of time, I will not believe it unless it is the man's capability to think about the answers of how's and why's. Man is a logical and a political animal, just as the great Aristotle thought we was. It was a very long time ago that Sir Isaac Newton questioned the falling apple that made him the discoverer of the concept of gravitational attraction, several decades later, this led us to the more comprehensive theory of space and time. Classical minds in the name of Archimedes, Newton, Einstein, Hawking, to name a few, throughout history, had unraveled the truth of universal laws of science. This means that the laws were true in all of the places on Earth and outside the planet, in all phenomena and events. By them, almost all of scientific doubts were answered by the laws, in which are describable and reproduceable by the use of Mathematics and Physics. The philosophical thoughts were gradually replaced by scientific analogies.

Throughout history, amidst the appreciation of the applications and understanding of discoveries, the understanding of the laws of science shuttered its place in the event of the entering of quantum physics, the new branch of science pertaining to the understanding of the behavior of sub-atomic particles within atoms. In these new laws defies the analogies of thinking as the rules were new to our minds, different from the present scientific laws. The present rules of science were immediately thrown out of the window.

In the present era, there are two ways representing the universe scientifically, the Theories of Relativity which governs the whole heavenly abyss, in our world and outside the galaxies, and the Quantum Physics which plays a vital role in the characteristics and behaviors of sub-atomic particles. The first is where our understanding of our universe is anchored from while the latter is new and revolutionary. Physicists are trying their ways to combine the two separate fields, which are now, still, seems impossible as they grow separately apart. The laws which we think are universal, made us to think again if truly universal or not.

Chapter 1

The Minute Universes

The Inward World Beyond the Vision's Proximity

"The energy produced by the breaking down of the atom is a very poor kind of thing. Anyone who expects a source of power from the transformation of these atoms is talking moonshine."

-Ernest Rutherford

It was a couple of minutes after I fell asleep that my mind started to wander through memories of mine. Then I saw myself as a young 8-year-old boy outside our classroom. It's a lunch break time in the typical hot sunny day.

"Childhood years were pretty boring for a kid who is too curious about the surroundings than his peers, as he is always observing nature in silence rather than joining others for a playtime to enjoy.", as the old man whispered as he noticed the kid staring at the colored rock under the shade. The young kid did not hear the words but myself.

Those were my years, I collected various types of rocks and pet little spiders, and when it's the time for them to lay eggs, I'm carefully observing them. As the eggs hatched, the little spiders are slowly moving out from the clumps of webs and feel the surroundings. I wonder, "How is the world for them to feel and realize?". "What is the world for minute creature really look like?" Until we head one step deeper, "What really like to live in microscopic surroundings or even atomic universes?" The space, too vast or too small, had left humans plenty of questions to answer.

In my elementary years, I had tapped by a book sitting in one of the shelves' corners of our library, the Encyclopedia Americana. While all my classmates were busy playing outside, seizing the free time after lunch. I am also busy reading alone at one of the tables inside. I gazed my eyes at those different types of rocks and pebbles with their different colors and textures really tickled my childhood imagination. I also wonder, if I collected these rocks, and positioned them symmetrically, will I open some magical portal or dimensions just like what I have seen in movies? The answer to my childlike question remained a mystery as I did not complete the rock groups stated in the book and found only a few numbers of it; marble, shale, slate and my favorite, pumice. Those rocks were scattered in our nearby yards in home and in school, the others were difficult to find.

Several centuries ago, someone think of an unusual idea: "If cutting a gold bar into pieces make it smaller, when is the time that it could not be cut anymore? And how small the pieces are? These first questions toward the understanding of the composition of everyday objects spread throughout curious minds of the era before the present scientific notions were established. A simpler question would be like this, "What is the smallest object in this world? And what are they composed of? Questioning the world scientifically is the first step to appreciate the laws of nature.

> Questioning the world scientifically is the first step to appreciate the laws of nature.

In elementary science, we are told that every object or matter in the universe were composed of clumps of tiny sphere-like structures called atoms. Thanks to the scientists behind the discoveries that we knew that already in an early age. We just don't appreciate it fully by our young conscious minds. Now that we have enough intellect to talk about it in a more scientific way, this is the time to face the knowledge. Every matter visible and invisible, were composed of combinations of different kinds of atoms. We were just a product of clumps of spherical entities that technically speaking, as old as the universe itself. As someone said, "If humans are composed of billions of atoms, then a scientist is a combination of atoms studying itself". The composition of matter is kind of indestructible, meaning that what comprises the neutron, proton, and electron, which are the three fundamental structures of an atom, cannot be easily divided or break apart into several new entities. We, as just like the world we live in, are just the composition of billions of atoms with different ratios of protons and neutrons clumped together to form matter. What comprises your pencil, your bag, the land you are standing, the air you breathe, and even the stars shining above you, are just the same entities comprising your body. Amongst the 118 elements in the periodic table your nearby school teaches you are the compositions of all the matter we can think or feel, all were composed from those basic elements.

> We, as just like the world we live in, are just the composition of billions of atoms with different ratios of protons and neutrons clumped together to form matter.

Now let's take a look at the series of elements described on the following paragraph. You can also look at the periodic table of elements as this was also a sequential list of types of atoms laid based on increasing number of protons in their nucleus, hence their atomic number. Organized by the Russian Chemist Dmitry Ivanovich Mendeleyev, this table is presently used to portray the best descriptions of the elements. In an element's stable state, the number of protons is equal to the number of its electrons. We can use this idea to determine the number of protons and electrons inside an atom.

The smallest atom, therefore, having an atomic number of 1 is the Hydrogen, a non-metal element discovered in 1766 by an English Physicist Henry Cavendish. Scientists had been producing it for years before it was recognized as an element. It has only a single proton as its nucleus, some types having an additional of 1 neutron as its isotope, and most of the cases, 1 valence electron sitting in its only shell. Its electron is called its valence electron as it is positioned in the outer shell of the atom. Hydrogen is known as the most abundant element in the universe.

The next larger element was Helium, a noble gas used in deep sea diving and on balloons for birthday parties. Scientists also used it for low temperature researches. This element was discovered in 1888 by the French Astronomer Jules Janssen. This element has two proton and in its stable state, has two electrons in its only shell, you can judge that this element is an insulator, as there are only two rooms for electrons in the first shell of any atom, there are no rooms left on Helium for outside electrons to fill in.

The next element is Lithium, the lightest among all the 118 elements; discovered in 1817 by a Swedish Chemist, Johan Arfwedson. This alkali metal is completely different than the first two. Having three protons and having two shells and three electrons, we can already know that this element is a conductor. The second shell of any atom can house 8 electrons in total, the first shell can accommodate two, therefore, there is one electron sitting in the second shell of Lithium and there are seven rooms for any outside electrons to come in. This structure of Lithium makes it an essential factor to include it in battery composition.

Figure 3. The two faces of carbon: Upper; the lead in pencil is made from a form of Carbon called graphite. Lower; a diamond is a solid form of Carbon with its atoms arranged in a crystal structure.

The fourth element in the periodic table is Beryllium. Discovered by Louis Vauquelin in 1798, it is an Alkali Earth Metal which is very reactive in nature. It is also considered a conductor having four electrons in total, two electrons in the first shell and another two electrons in its second shell. Its valence electron is also two, as there two electrons in its outer shell.

The next element is Boron, a non-reactive metalloid. Discovered in 1808 by a series of names, the French Chemists, Joseph Louis Gay Lussac, Louis Jaques Thenard and the English Chemist Sir Humphry Davy. This element houses 5 protons in total hence can accommodate 5 electrons in its stable state. There are three electrons in its second shell that's why its valence electrons are three.

The sixth element is something famous, carbon, a non-metal discovered by sir Antoine Lavoisier. Its atomic number is six that's why its protons is also six. It was discovered in ancient times and the discovery year was unknown. It is a dull black in color in a form of graphite but hard and transparent in the form of diamond. Carbon houses four electrons in its second shell that's why the valence electrons are four. Because there are only 8 room for the second shell and the Carbon's second shell was half-filled. This element is considered to be a semi-conductor.

The seventh element is the Nitrogen. Its discoverer was a Chemist and a Physician named Daniel Rutherford in 1772. Nitrogen is a non-metal element essential for living organisms as it is needed for protein and used for fertilizer. At the same time, it is commonly used in plastic making and explosives. Having seven protons surrounded by 2 electrons, there are five electrons in its second shell. Therefore, there are 3 remaining "empty rooms" for other electrons to come in. With this, this element is considered to be an insulator.

The eight element is something what we, humans are needed in order to survive; to breath in oxygen. It was discovered the same year as Nitrogen by a Swedish Chemist, Carl Wilhelm Scheele. The element was also discovered in 1774 by an English Chemist, Joseph Priestly. He published his findings the same year, three years earlier than Scheele. Due to that, Priestly is now widely known for the discoverer of oxygen. Oxygen has its fully filled first shell with two electrons in it.

At the same time, it has the second shell filled with six electrons leaving two rooms for other electrons.

The ninth element is Fluorine. Its first shell is filled with two electrons and its second shell having seven electrons, leaving two rooms for outside electrons to passed through or enter. Its discoverer is the French Chemist Henri Moissan in 1886.

The tenth, Neon, one of the perfect insulators. It shells are fully filled. Take note that the first shell only houses two electrons and the second, only eight. It glows red in color when an electrical discharge is passed through it. It was discovered by two British Chemists, Sir William Ramsay and Morris Travers in 1898.

Now from the tenth element, we will jump to the largest element listed in the periodic table, the Oganesson, also known as Ununoctium, A noble gas type discovered in 2006. All of its six shells are full and its 7th shell houses 8 electrons garnering 118 electrons in total as its atomic number.

To fully grasp the systematic pattern denoting the number of electrons and the shells, further look at the table below. Well, it's kind of systematized at first but the numbers soon to be more complicated as the atomic numbers are increasing. Maybe you, the readers can solve for the general equation describing the number of each electron in each shell in every element.

Table 1. Showing the Number of Electrons in its Shells of each Element

Element Name/ Atomic number	Number of electrons in each shell						
	1st shell	2nd shell	3rd shell	4th shell	5th shell	6th shell	7th shell
Hydrogen, 1	1						
Helium, 2	2						
Lithium, 3	2	1					
Beryllium, 4	2	2					
Boron, 5	2	3					

Table 1. Showing the Number of Electrons in its Shells of each Element

Element Name/ Atomic number	Number of electrons in each shell						
	1st shell	2nd shell	3rd shell	4th shell	5th shell	6th shell	7th shell
Carbon, 6	2	4					
Nitrogen, 7	2	5					
Oxygen, 8	2	6					
Fluorine, 9	2	7					
Neon, 10	2	8					
Sodium, 11	2	8	1				
Magnesium, 12	2	8	2				
Aluminum, 13	2	8	3				
Silicon, 14	2	8	4				
Phosphorous, 15	2	8	5				
Sulfur, 16	2	8	6				
Chlorine, 17	2	8	7				
Argon, 18	2	8	8				
Potassium, 19	2	8	8	1			
Calcium, 20	2	8	8	2			
Scandium, 21	2	8	9	2			
Titanium, 22	2	8	10	2			
Vanadium, 23	2	8	11	2			
Chromium, 24	2	8	13	1			
Manganese, 25	2	8	13	2			
Iron, 26	2	8	14	2			
Cobalt, 27	2	8	15	2			
Nickel, 28	2	8	16	2			
Copper, 29	2	8	18	1			
Zinc, 30	2	8	18	2			
Gallium, 31	2	8	18	3			
Germanium, 32	2	8	18	4			

Table 1. Showing the Number of Electrons in its Shells of each Element

Element Name/ Atomic number	Number of electrons in each shell						
	1st shell	2nd shell	3rd shell	4th shell	5th shell	6th shell	7th shell
Arsenic, 33	2	8	18	5			
Selenium, 34	2	8	18	6			
Bromine, 35	2	8	18	7			
Krypton, 36	2	8	18	8			
Rubidium, 37	2	8	18	8	1		
Strontium, 38	2	8	18	8	2		
Yttrium, 39	2	8	18	9	2		
Zirconium, 40	2	8	18	10	2		
Niobium, 41	2	8	18	12	1		
Molybdenum, 42	2	8	18	13	1		
Technetium, 43	2	8	18	13	2		
Ruthenium, 44	2	8	18	15	1		
Rhodium, 45	2	8	18	16	1		
Palladium, 46	2	8	18	18	0		
Silver, 47	2	8	18	18	1		
Cadmium, 48	2	8	18	18	2		
Indium, 49	2	8	18	18	3		
Tin, 50	2	8	18	18	4		
Antimony, 51	2	8	18	18	5		
Tellurium, 52	2	8	18	18	6		
Iodine, 53	2	8	18	18	7		
Xenon, 54	2	8	18	18	8		
Cesium, 55	2	8	18	18	8	1	
Barium, 56	2	8	18	18	8	2	
Lanthanum, 57	2	8	18	18	9	2	
Cerium, 58	2	8	18	19	9	2	
Praseodymium, 59	2	8	18	21	8	2	
Neodymium, 60	2	8	18	22	8	2	

Table 1. Showing the Number of Electrons in its Shells of each Element

Element Name/ Atomic number	Number of electrons in each shell						
	1st shell	2nd shell	3rd shell	4th shell	5th shell	6th shell	7th shell
Promethium, 61	2	8	18	23	8	2	
Samarium, 62	2	8	18	24	8	2	
Europium, 63	2	8	18	25	8	2	
Gadolinium, 64	2	8	18	25	9	2	
Terbium, 65	2	8	18	27	8	2	
Dysprosium, 66	2	8	18	28	8	2	
Holmium, 67	2	8	18	29	8	2	
Erbium, 68	2	8	18	30	8	2	
Thulium, 69	2	8	18	31	8	2	
Ytterbium, 70	2	8	18	32	8	2	
Lutetium, 71	2	8	18	32	9	2	
Hafnium, 72	2	8	18	32	10	2	
Tantalium, 73	2	8	18	32	11	2	
Tungsten, 74	2	8	18	32	12	2	
Rhenium, 75	2	8	18	32	13	2	
Osmium, 76	2	8	18	32	14	2	
Iridium, 77	2	8	18	32	15	2	
Platinum, 78	2	8	18	32	17	1	
Gold, 79	2	8	18	32	18	1	
Mercury, 80	2	8	18	32	18	2	
Thallium, 81	2	8	18	32	18	3	
Lead, 82	2	8	18	32	18	4	
Bismuth, 83	2	8	18	32	18	5	
Polonium, 84	2	8	18	32	18	6	
Astatine, 85	2	8	18	32	18	7	
Radon, 86	2	8	18	32	18	8	
Francium, 87	2	8	18	32	18	8	1

Table 1. Showing the Number of Electrons in its Shells of each Element

Element Name/ Atomic number	Number of electrons in each shell						
	1st shell	2nd shell	3rd shell	4th shell	5th shell	6th shell	7th shell
Radium, 88	2	8	18	32	18	8	2
Actinium, 89	2	8	18	32	18	9	2
Thorium, 90	2	8	18	32	18	10	2
Protactinium, 91	2	8	18	32	20	9	2
Uranium, 92	2	8	18	32	21	9	2
Neptunium, 93	2	8	18	32	22	9	2
Plutonium, 94	2	8	18	32	24	8	2
Americium, 95	2	8	18	32	25	8	2
Curium, 96	2	8	18	32	25	9	2
Berkelium, 97	2	8	18	32	27	8	2
Californium, 98	2	8	18	32	28	8	2
Einsteinium, 99	2	8	18	32	29	8	2
Fermium, 100	2	8	18	32	30	8	2
Mendelevium, 101	2	8	18	32	31	8	2
Nobelium, 102	2	8	18	32	32	8	2
Lawrencium, 103	2	8	18	32	32	8	3
Rutherfordium, 104	2	8	18	32	32	10	2
Dubnium, 105	2	8	18	32	32	11	2
Seaborgium, 106	2	8	18	32	32	12	2
Bohrium, 107	2	8	18	32	32	13	2
Hassium, 108	2	8	18	32	32	14	2
Meitnerium, 109	2	8	18	32	32	15	2
Darmstadtium, 110	2	8	18	32	32	16	2
Roentgenium, 111	2	8	18	32	32	17	2
Copernicium, 112	2	8	18	32	32	18	2
Nihonium, 113	2	8	18	32	32	18	3
Flerovium, 114	2	8	18	32	32	18	4

Table 1. Showing the Number of Electrons in its Shells of each Element

Element Name/ Atomic number	Number of electrons in each shell						
	1st shell	2nd shell	3rd shell	4th shell	5th shell	6th shell	7th shell
Ununpentium, 115	2	8	18	32	32	18	5
Livermorium, 116	2	8	18	32	32	18	6
Tennessine, 117	2	8	18	32	32	18	7
Ununoctium, 118	2	8	18	32	32	18	8

It seems and we know that the strongest dominating entity are those of the largest in size: the large heavy tanks of the Russian Army, the colossal-sized ships at the Panama Canal, and the big heavyweight grizzly bears roaming the forests: in the present era, the largest in size are the strongest of kind. But we are slowly realizing that in the minute universes, as small as the neutron itself, holds the most powerful force of the universe, the nuclear energy. Lurking in the midst of minute spaces, the one of the tangible entities roaming every atom in the universe has the most destroying force amongst the list of explosives. The smallest in size is now the most destructive entities ever known to man.

Figure 4. Dmitri Ivanovich Mendeleev is a Russian chemist and inventor. He is best known for formulating the Periodic Law and creating a version of the periodic table of elements.

Chapter 2

The Bizarre World of Sub-atomics

The Universe Outside the Classical Laws of Nature

"God doesn't play dice with the universe"

-Albert Einstein

> *"From the sunny day outside, my dream put me in a dark yet spacious room. I could barely touch anything, and only hears strange sounds from something beyond.*
>
> *"Where am I and why I am in this place?" my heart is pounding and I am starting to feel the fright. I could barely explore the dark room and I just want to wake. Little did I know that my dream put me inside of an atom from a rock I am staring to. It was a very frightening moment.*

After the discovery that all matter comprises of elements embodied by a set of rules of chemical science, people as being driven by curiosity want to go deeper after the atom. Numerous questions were raised and composed to what is really the inside of each element. What comprises the atom? And what comprises the entity comprising the atom? Or in general sense, what is matter really made up of? At those times, people tend to study inwardly deeper on the minute scales of matter than the outside realm of vast universe.

From the outer scales of an atom, we are heading one step deeper. Atoms are made up of just three entities, the proton and neutron fixed in the center and the electron wandering around it. Beside those three is an empty space filling the entirety of the inside. In general, atoms are made mostly of space, almost 99.999999% and the proton, neutron and electron only amount to 0.000001%. The values are not finely accurate, it's just the way to show that atoms are mostly filled up of space. The three entities were so small that if a nucleus is a size of a marble, the atom it belonged would be the size of a football ground! From this analogy, we can state that every matter, including you and me and this living

environment, in microscale, is just made up of almost spaces! In fact, if we could detach all of the spaces from all the atoms in our world, that would fit inside a single sugar cube!

The fact that everything relates deeper beyond the microscales, opens up various questions our conscious minds are in hunger. Some questions are like this, "If everything is made of atoms and its compositions, does it tell us that energy is deeply rooted to sub-atomic worlds? The answers to this question are finely and accurately

Figure 5. Peter Ware Higgs is a British theoretical physicist, professor at the University of Edinburg, a Nobel laureate in Physics for his work on the mass of subatomic particles, and the discoverer of Higgs Boson particle.

understood nowadays, in the era of nuclear science. The time that human competitiveness went

beyond the limits of conscience and had used their capability to invent a destructible equipment; the nuclear bomb, killed more than a hundred of thousands of civilians, mostly women and children. Nowadays, the world had learned and saw the effects of that destruction, that whoever holds that machine seems to be the silent grizzly tiger waiting for its bad mood to make a death wish. Somebody somehow, must create an international policy to monitor, control and prevent any signs of mad dilemma.

Nuclear energy does not have to be destructible in nature, we must just control the explosions to convert it to something essential, electricity. Nuclear Power Plants nowadays had produced millions of powers in the developed countries especially in the U.S., and continue to provide cheap and affordable electricity in the market. Just like fire, nuclear energy is something we can treat as a friend and a foe.

> Just like fire, nuclear energy is something we can treat as a friend and as a foe.

So, what is really the composition of protons, neutrons, and electrons? To find out the answer, scientists started to smash or put these particles into collisions, and detect what the resulting body will produce. One of these collision machines is the LHC or Large Hadron Collider, located across the border of France and Switzerland, the most powerful accelerator in the world. The machine accelerates the proton so fast closing at the speed of light then collided by another proton. The collision will produce remnants of the broken particles. There are no other ways to break apart proton but to put them in collision. In this technique, scientists discovered plenty of smaller and smaller particles comprising the proton such as the Higgs Boson and several quarks which creates another table for smaller particles known as the Standard Model. Nowadays, the list of smaller particles in the Standard Model comes more complicated than the Periodic Table of Elements.

There are several theories arises from the discovery of smaller particles. One of these is the String Theory proposed by the famous New York University professor and a theoretical physicist, Michio Kaku. He concluded that amongst the number of new particles and their different properties, there are a general law which are

Figure 6. Michio Kaku is an American Physicist, futurologist, writer of popular science books, a professor of theoretical Physics at City College of New York and CUNY Graduate Center and the co-creator of String Theory.

governing them all. He said, that if we could break down one step smaller those smaller particles, we could conceptualize that the resulting entity will be like that of a small short string. Just like a rubber band which ripples and vibrates at a specific frequency producing wavelengths and energy to form matter. He theorized that each frequency and wavelengths constitute for a specific particle. Each frequency and wavelength then producing energy denotes a specific property of a particle. If that will be proven to be true, then matter in this entire observable universe could be made up of clumps of strings vibrating differently or in unison creating matter. That would make a totally different perspective on the origin of matter and energy and will greatly revolutionize all of the present scientific notions of science.

If String Theory will be proven to be true, then matter in this entire observable universe could be made up of clumps of strings vibrating differently or in unison creating matter.

Chapter 3

Within a Blue Planet

The Advancement of Technology Inside the Spherical Space-Ship

"The Earth is what we all have in common"

-Wendell Berry

"*I am nearly in suffocation pulling my breath when I escaped the dream and awaken. The storm was ended and the sun which is slowly rising began to exposed itself in the midst above. My dreams were calm at first but became frightening at the end especially on that dark spacious room. As I started to hear the joyful noises of the children outside, I decided to get up and make up my beddings.*"

"*I went to kitchen and make a cup of coffee. Every sip gives my mind a kick start. When I am fully awake and conscious about my surroundings, I decided to go to the balcony and feel the ambiance outside. It was a Saturday morning and the kids are having fun playing. Together with random people who are busy walking, the sounds of vehicles and the noises of laughter and conversations are giving that day a lively start.*"

"*I live in my dormitory several kilometers from the middle of the city, just like several students and employees, we have the same situation from weekdays to weekends; the city's weekly routine. This is the city life, like the other lives in any other cities, this is the world we live in, our life in this spherical blue planet.*"

Amongst hundreds of planets residing the Milky Way, there could no other planet as of now that can support life except Earth; the planet placed thirdly from the sun, next to Venus and before Mars. This planet is orbited by its only satellite, Moon which in turn if translated into Latin, Luna, the farthest heavenly body ever set foot by man. In this bluish average sized planet resides roughly 8 billion people and counting, few of them asking the same questions over and over again in their head, "what is really up there?", the question of uncertainty. Together with various forms of life and matter, Earth must be old enough to sustain the evolution. Existed roughly 4.543 billion years ago, this planet is fortunate to exist in the midst of danger in the outer space.

> Luna, the Earth's only satellite, was the farthest heavenly body ever set foot by man.

Once to contain single massive boulder of land, the Pangea, the latter broke apart to seven large continents presented in queue according to size; Australia, Europe, Antarctica, South America, North America, Africa and Asia. The list started on the smallest land scale up to the largest. These houses different forms of living and non-living organisms arose from land. Hundreds of thousands of different types of living entities ranging from the smallest bacteria to the deadliest fungi, and up to the largest mammal existing at present time, blue whales. As a matter of fact, 99.9% of animals were gone extinct before humans came to life. Although, that represents almost all of animals living in nature, the numbers remaining are still numerous. Some animals got

their names after becoming extinct for several years, and some, were not yet to be discovered. All wside variety of creatures were residing inside the rotating world of oblate spheroid shaped planet capable of sustaining the continuity of life. We, humans are living in here several centuries ago until now, and hoping several centuries to the far-fetched future.

In this planet is where most of the laws of Physics were discovered, through the ages of time, through the lengthiness of generations and through the efforts of human minds to understand the behaviors of all observable phenomena. Humans invented a way to record ideas and concepts as the years go by; the systematic form of writing, for the benefit and use of future generations. By that primitive technology, the developments garnered by a specified number of people were handed over to other places easily and carried over to their siblings. Ideas were mainly preserved and developed by the use of writing. And that is where generations strived and conquered the possibility of human extinction.

Above all creatures, humans are the only specie that can adapt and improve easily from the changing environment. As a matter of fact, you can see peoples' lives in the midst of squeezing temperatures of Alaska. You can find people travelling by their camels in the scorching hotness of deserts of Kalahari and Sahara. From the slums of Africa and Bangladesh, to the lavish living in San Francisco and the U.S., people are around the world living their lives and their daily routine already adapted to their environment.

This planet is rich in histories. Stories that are very unforgettable that it plays major roles in succeeding generations. Each perspective of each people had their own stories untold or shared once in their lifetime. By the essence of severity, this planet witnessed two world wars. The first, by chemical warfare and the second, by nuclear energy and there were numerous historic local wars recorded.

> Above all creatures, humans are the only specie that can adapt and improve easily from the changing environment.

Among all the living species, we were the only one who can develop modern technologies. Humans are so clever up to the extent that they can do massive boulders of explosions to finish their enemies and win the war.

I, the author of this book, is living in this planet for 27 long years. This planet witnessed my survival from being a toddler up to being a fully grown working human. This planet saw how I garnered a good education from a nearby school, witnessed how I got my degree up until living my career. Well, my story is not different from the others, as a matter of fact, almost all of us are following the lifetime routine; get a good education, go to work, and get a good life from it, which is everybody's system.

Amongst the numerous histories of this planet that we can clearly predict where it is heading; to advance in technology and scientific endeavor, creating numerous laws and discover plenty of new sciences to understand the general concept of nature and the universe. Humans were the only specie capable for this challenge and we are always on the process of improvement. We are blessed to have the capability but unfortunately, having limited senses to interact with the world.

The world's greatest technological advancements were famously grouped into four eras. The industrial revolution, the time in which engines and machines were invented. Producing the concept of generators, motors, and other machineries to carry out the big tasks easier and with the help of minimum labor force. There was a boom on the transportation business such as the invention of railway trains and engine cars. The generation and distribution of electricity was also made easily possible creating the efforts for electric distribution systems, life would never be the same after the development of electrical machineries. This era created more jobs for the people unlike any other but on the other hand, eliminated some. Industrial era made us to realize that machines greatly contributed to the world's advancement, we are made to be dependent on machines since the industrial period.

The second historic period of the world is the digital age, where the computers and electronics come from behind the scene to minimize the efforts of the corporate worlds. The organization of data, faster computing,storing big chunks of information and automatic processing were one of the major advantages of the development of computers. Telecommunication were at high stakes at this period eliminating the need to do manually written words and wait for the mailman to arrive, the messaging took only seconds to come in. The corporate business world also greatly benefited in the digital period. The massive amounts of data of the sales revenue of a company as well as other matters such as the status of each its employee, their salary wages, and other figures constitutes for a need of a storing device and that's where the computers are coming in.

Next is something of a result of the digital age, the information period; where massive amounts of information are now available to the public. In this age is where our younger version had witnessed. The development of the social media, websites and other online flatforms for entertainment, information, and other purposes constitute a massive dispersion of information amongst the public. Numerous people exploited the chances of transferring their business to this cyberspace and succeed. Others were suffering to the dark sides such as the invasion of privacy, personal information leakage and security. Each period has their benefits and advantages and on other hand of the coin, their dark sides being exploited by many. And now, our present era, several years after the start of the twentieth century, the artificial intelligence period. The development of the artificial intelligence or AI is one the most exciting period of the modern world. This is the time where humans are now having their counterpart to think, evaluate, decide and do their job completely. This is where our minds are getting challenged. Some fears to be eliminated from the economy and some are just excited to use it for technological potency.

Figure 7. The Iconic Pictures of Industrial Age

Some are fearing to the rise of self-thinking robots not just because they do their job independently but to a deeper extent like wiping out the human kind. Tech billionaire such as Elon Musk and other giants on the use of AI are now in the lead to where this age is going. One thing is for sure, despite of the negative effects of every historical development period, to where it will lead is always going to prevail.

Chapter 4

The Vastness of the Realm of Space

The Extent of the Fabric's Limit

"One in 200 stars has habitable earth-like planets surrounding it. In the galaxy, half a billion stars have earth-like planets going around them, that's huge, half a billion! So, when we look at the night sky, it makes sense that someone is looking back to us."

-Michio Kaku

> "*As I am looking at the kids outside, playing and teasing, not being competitively with each other but just having fun. I began reminiscing my childhood, I am also fond of playing with my friends, but prefers to play only with myself. I remembered that one time, when it was my birthday, I wished something for my gift, it's not a toy, or any collectibles but a small calculator. My mother gave to me a small cheap one and witnessed my happy smiles. She likes to give me jigsaw puzzles to solve as well as the rubik's cube aside from blocks and Legos. Those brain challenging toys helped me a lot to aspire to think at my young age, and molded me in my student years.*"

"In my childhood, I am always fascinated when I look upon the stars twinkling in the night in the midst of darkness above. My mind was wondering, "What was the feeling of getting to those places?", "What would be those places like?". The curiosity had produced upon my head such questions of mine. "If you have the power to travel anywhere, where would you go?" I bet someone would say that they would go to the beautiful beaches in America, or in other lavish countryside, or maybe to Japan, Korea, and other developed countries. But my childhood mind was different if I have to answer that question, "I would like to go beyond the outer space, to those stars twinkling above, to the emptiness of the darkness of the outside of our planet, and want to know what would be my feelings if I look back behind." "I guess that would be more exciting."

It is true that there are numerous types of worlds out there lurking in the dark the light had missed to shine. This proved the fact that space is so vast enough that it can't entirely covered by light. The universe is wide, and continuously increasing its boundaries through time. To visualize the speed of this entity, we must learn the essence of what we call a "light year". But imagining how fast light travels is a prerequisite of that subject. Travelling in a swift 299,792,458 meters per second, that fixed speed is the maximum limit all matter can travel through space. Nothing travels faster than light speed even the most powerful engines can't surpass this boundary. It's the nature's cardinal sin; "Thou shall not travel faster than light."

> Nothing travels faster than light speed even the most powerful engines can't surpass this boundary.

To visualize the speed of light, just imagine that it can take just 1.3 seconds of travel time from Earth to its moon. Our sun is about 150,000,000 km. but that lengthiness only takes approximately 8 minutes and 17 seconds travel time of light to reach the surface of Earth. Each foot of distance only took for about 1 nanosecond for light to pass through and only 3.3 nanoseconds for 1 meter. Just visualize how light scattered in the room after we click the switch, that is so immensely fast! The constancy of light's speed indeed is the true secret of nature.

Although the speed of light is the upper limit of everything's movement, it can't boast to travel in a blink within the vastness of the universe. The vast outer space is so immeasurable that scientists were forced to made the term "light year" to describe the distance a light travel in 1 Earth year! This means that 1 light year equals to 5,875,000,000,000 miles! This is a tremendous distance to begin the measurements. In fact, it takes 70,000 years for light to travel the nearest galaxy from us. And it takes light approximately 4 hours from Earth to reach Pluto. Although light is in its blinking speed, it is technically slow when travelling to the vastness of the entirety of the universe.

> Although light is in its blinking speed, it is technically slow when travelling to the vastness of the entirety of the universe.

The universe as scientists think is like a giant balloon with insects glued on its surface. The insects represent every galaxy residing the outer space and the balloon, the spaces in the universe. Now, the balloon grew bigger and continuously growing. Hence, the insects will move away from each other in the balloon without even moving in their actual position. The same in our universe. Galaxies are moving away from their neighboring ones. This implies the fact that the space in our universe is increasing through time. The space is affected with some forces blowing it up from its center, or maybe at the point of the Big Bang. If this continues to happen, the stars, and other galaxies will fade out in the night sky sometime in the future, due to their vast growing distance from us. The night sky at that time will be totally dark and only shines by the moon, the twinkling of the stars will be not visible anymore.

> Sometime in the future, the twinkling of the stars will be permanently not visible anymore.

But although all galaxies are moving away toward another, there is still a force pulling them altogether. This force is gradually decreasing as the distance between them increases. Also known as the Newton's Law of Gravitation, states that every matter experience a force with each other that is equal to the product of their masses divided by the square of the distance between them. Portrayed in the mathematical formula: **F = GMm/d^2,** where **F** is the gravitational force, **G** is the gravitational constant, **M** is the mass of one object, **m** is the mass of another and **d,** the distance between them. The gravitational constant, **G** is equal to 6.67×10^{-11} Newtons/kg^2*m^2. This means that the nearer two objects are, the greater the force of attraction between them, the farther them apart, the lesser. The generality of this law is so monumental that it is still applicable in the world of atoms.

Implying that equation, we could go back at this book's introduction stating that the space is not nothingness. Actually, if there was a force between every matter in the universe, even the farthest ones, (you and the rock in the Jupiter's soil) there will be a medium connecting them. This implies and confirms that the space is not nothingness but the medium of propagation that is used to transfer forces. Every object in the universe including us is connected by space.

"The universe is increasing." That phrase once sent shockwaves to the curious minds of the modern era. If the universe is ever increasing in size, so fast that even the light from the edge of space needs thousands if not millions of years to reach the lenses of our powerful binoculars, where we are in the vast volume of space? We can't also comprehend the fact the if the universe's size is increasing, this means that the space itself is stretching if not created continuously to make such increase. And if ever we had our luck to catch the edge of space, and outrun it, what will be the world outside its dominion? And if ever, there is something in it arises hundreds of questions and discoveries for our minds to comprehend. Space, a synonym for emptiness, could hold more something than the word "empty" itself.

Figure 8. Isaac Newton, an English Scientist who contributed significantly to the field of science over his lifetime. He invented calculus and provided a clear understanding of optics. But his most significant work had to do with forces, and specifically with the development of a universal law of gravitation and his laws of motion.

Chapter 5

The World of Multiverses

The Universe in Another Dimension

"I believe we exist in a multiverse of universes."

-Michio Kaku

"It is very important to realize and appreciate our position and situation in this world. We are just one of the lucky species in this universe who happen to survive numerous challenges of extinction, as we are always in the verge of it. Although, we are higher species amongst numerous living things, we still are powerless compare to the vastness of the universe. Our senses and abilities to perceive our environment is limited, there are indeed worlds out there beyond our perceptions. After all, we are just blessed to experience our Lord's grand design."

"Although this world is full of unpredictable events and chaos, unfair systems and social tensions, this is the most practical and convenient place to live. This is our spaces, where our senses are capable to see and experience the physical and other aspects of our existence."

"Although science tells that the Earth is the only habitable planet in the solar system or at least for now, some discoveries suggests that there might be other worlds that sustain a living environment in some period in the history of time. But amongst several theories of another Earth-like planets thrived in the past, some argue that maybe it is not the Earth-like we must find, maybe the living environment lives not in our worlds, but in another dimensions."

What do we immediately think when we heard the word "dimension"? Here, we have multiple meanings of that word and each description differs from another greatly. In the world of mathematics and science, that word mainly describe two different entities. In the language of numbers, dimension is the measurements of the physical sense of an object. It's height, width and length are telling the object's physiques and so its dimension. In this world, we can either go in all directions, climbing up or going down, left and right, and forward and backward, those directions are the representations of our three-dimensional world. In layman's, the descriptions of how big or small an object is, how flat or curved it may seem, is its dimensional identity.

That word's description tells a different story in the language of science. "Dimension" in scientific term is directly the world we live in, not merely the physical appearance but the entirety of its essences. The entirety of our world in the views of human perception is our dimension.

Figure 9. One of the interesting questions in Physics is "What is the other dimensions look like?" or "Is it really existing?"

The theories that gave rise to the possibilities of the existence of multiverses began at the very point of the discovery of the new branch of modern science, the study of sub-atomic particles, the quantum physics. It is always stated in the entirety of this book that there are three fundamental particles comprises the atom: the proton, neutron and the electron, which is the composition of all the matter in the universe. Among the two, the latter has its mobility to travel freely in the fabric of space and has unusual properties that seems to violate the existing laws of science. The bizarre encounter began when scientists discovered that the electron can vanish and exist in space, or even exist in two places at the same time! This discovery brings such an extraordinary event in the history of physics and opened several doubts and propositions to question the workings of nature that in some time, gave rise to the idea of the possible existence of multiverses.

> The entirety of our world in the views of human perception is our dimension.

The first idea that served to be a great contender to open doors to the existence of multiverses is the unusual behaviors of electron. "If electron can vanish and exist in space, does another sub-atomic particle like proton and neutron can do it?". If other particle can, meaning, we are all vanishing in a blink and then exist at the same point in space every time! (Take note of the word "same point") If all of the particles in the universe vanish and exist at a very fast similar rate, how can we detect to prove this idea, as our senses and instruments comprised by atoms also vanish and exist similarly? Humans had detected this scheme on electron due to the fact that electron vanish and exist in a different rate than any other particles presently visible to us under powerful instruments. Again, if this idea is proven to be true, then we can entirely expect that at the moment every particle vanishes, there are different worlds and universes exist at the same points in space, those that having alternate frequency of vanish and exist scheme, and immediately vanish once we exist in space again. It would be a very different and exciting universe, who knows?

> If electron can vanish and exist in space, does another sub-atomic particle like proton and neutron can do it?

The proposal idea that every atom comprising every matter in the universe vanish and exist in a blink at the same rate continuously through time is astounding and radical but difficult to prove. This open numerous possibilities of the existence of other universes beyond our realm of perception. At present time, the world doesn't know how to prove it, we would wait for a certain time that a small tweak of change occurs in the vanish-exist rate so that we may detect it. When? The answer is we don't know. The world may wait for the next hundreds of years or so after the successes in numerous advancements of technologies to alter the world of this radical idea. Maybe you can solve this challenge and be the next Einstein and Newton of your generation!

The latter idea that permits the possibilities to exist another matter with the spaces consumed by another doesn't violate the Law of Impenetrability, that states that "No two matter occupies the same space at the same time". If the vanish and exist scheme was true, matter can share the same space but not the same time, as two matters are having different rates of vanishing and existing. This is somewhat a radical idea answering the question, "Is multiverses can be found outside our realm of space, or it is existing within our present spaces?".

Some theoretical minds also believed that multiverses don't exist within us in the present time, but existing outside the boundary of our physical universe; This is the second idea or propositions on the possible existence of multiverses. Those places were in physique too to experience by our senses, but the massive and vast distance serves as the great hindrances for us human to reach those places. The lengthiness of distance of those universes can't ever reach by our own light as those were also moving away from us. Those universes may portray different laws of their sciences, different compositions of their structures, and various numbers of new systems and creatures. At some time, do you ever think of what is happening to some creature while existing in those places?

The idea that multiverses may exist outside the boundary of our physical reach comes from the two pillars of the law of science, the Theory of Relativity and the Quantum Physics. Relativity theories founded by Mr. Albert Einstein, is the law of heavenly bodies, including gravity and the concept of time.

Figure 10. Stephen Hawking was regarded as one of the most brilliant theoretical physicists of the modern era. He made several contributions to science such as developed theories on the creation of the universe and furthered our understanding on black holes, stars and other heavenly bodies.

One of his famous equation, **E=mc^2** dictates the equivalency of matter and energy. The **E** stands for energy, the **m** for the mass of a given matter and the variable **c,** the speed of light itself. Any matter just weighing several grams can give off enormous amounts of energy due to the value of the square of speed of light. This in turn means that every matter possesses massive amounts of potential energy just waiting to unlock. Einstein also improved our understanding on gravity as Sir Isaac Newton theorized that gravity is a kind of force pulling two entities together but didn't succeed to explain what those forces are. The equation **F=GMm/d^2** also regarded as inverse square law was stated earlier in chapter 4 of this book. That equation governs and predicts the movement of planets, stars, comets and other entities in the universe. Einstein also was the first person to conjoined the terms space and time in one scientific persona. Yielding to the formation of the fourth dimension in space, time, as it is relative to which observer is looking and measuring to. Pertaining to heavenly bodies, the Theory of Relativity is the contender to explain the workings of the universe.

In terms of intellectual capability, humans were made ahead of all the species in the animal kingdom. In fact, the present generations of humans were considerably smarter than our ancestors hundreds of years ago. We think differently, we are made to question logic, test hypothesis, and ask the least obvious to understand our lives and our world. Scientifically, we run numerous tests of experiments out of curiosity, to understand the how's and why's of the workings of everyday surroundings. Blessed by thinking capacity, human's biological designs were not made to sense the full experience of the environment.

> Blessed by thinking capacity, human's biological designs were not made to sense the full experience of the environment.

Remember that our vision, considered by many to be the most important senses of human being, is light dependent. We can't see what surrounds us in the darkness. We need light to sense and use our vision. And even with the presence of light, our eyes cannot see the entire light's spectrum. Human eyes can only see a fraction of it as being called the "visible light", around 380 to 700 nanometers of wavelength. There are a long arrays of radio waves, infrared, gamma rays and numerous more that are still invincible to our vision. We had only several numbers of arrangements of colors existing due to the thin line of our senses' accessibility to light. The distant object can be seen as blurry due to the limitations of our vision's capacity to see. Among all, our vision is just capable to see and perceive just a tiny amount of information of our living environment.

Our hearing ability, the same as the latter, cannot hear all of the frequencies in space. Amidst the long array of frequencies, our ear is designed to hear around 20hz to 20khz just enough to facilitate a conversation. Anymore sounds louder than 20khz or softer than 20hz or infrasound were laid down beyond our reach of perception. In that dilemma, it could be true that there are numerous sounds out there that we couldn't hear for the rest of our lives. Considering the limitations of our two most important senses for perception, do you still not believe on the concept of other worlds of multiverses? Worlds in another dimension may exist in our present spaces, we just could not perceive the experience due to the limitations of our senses.

> Worlds in another dimension may exist in our present spaces, we just could not perceive the experience due to the limitations of our senses.

Glossary of Terms

Atom – the smallest collective entity comprising a matter; it has several parts and sub-atomic composition that makes up everything in the universe, living and non-living.

Black Hole – merely the absence of the fabric of space in a particular place in the universe. Typically resides in the center of every galaxy.

Brain – a lightweight soft membrane inside the skull which is responsible for any logical reasoning and knowledge acquired and developed by its beholder. Any thoughts, imaginations, ideas and propositions are all crafted and created by someone who has the brain capacity to execute it.

Big Bang Theory – a creational theory proposes that the universe from the beginning of time was compressed in a very tiny entity in the midst of darkness and later dominated the entirety of space after a gigantic explosion.

Charge – the unit pertaining to the energy and direction of the magnetic field stored within the three elementary particles, the electron, proton and the neutron.

Color – a photographic representation of the effect of wavelengths to human eyes' perception as different wavelengths constitute its corresponding color.

Corpuscle Theory – the proposition of Mr. Isaac Newton that pertains to the idea of light being 100% elastic luminous entities bouncing and wandering around the space providing such plain sight of lighted areas.

Coulomb – the unit of charge of either an electron or proton or both.

Darkness – occurs when there is an absence of visible light; not merely the nothingness but the absence of light perceivable by the naked eye.

Dimension – the physical attributes of a particular solid entity pertaining to height, length and width or x, y and z measurements in a Cartesian plane.

Distance – the length of one-dimensional space from one point to another pertaining to how far or near two entities are in space.

Double Slit Experiment – an experiment on sub-atomic particles set to produce or show the two natures of light; its wave and particle duality.

Earth – the name of our planet; the only planet in our solar system that harbors life and other living activities; the third planet from the sun.

Efficiency – mathematically, the percentage of the ratio of any output with its input within the system. The indications of how well a particular system utilizes energy.

Electron – a part of the atom that wanders around the nucleus; responsible entity for the existence of electricity.

Element – any of the 118 elements in the periodic table which consist of different atomic structure, properties, and behaviors.

Energy – a quantitative property transferrable to entities or in a system recognizable in the performance of workin the form of heat and light.

Extinction – the case where the generations of living species of animals and plants are being wiped out due to various types of destructions and other phenomena.

Experiment – a meticulous process of doing something to acquire result for data gathering, theory development, and discover something as intended or not.

Free Electron – is the excess electron in an atoms structure thus, easily swayed or moved by external magnetic field or by the collision with another electron.

Frequency – the term pertaining to the number of times a specific event occurs in a specified length of time usually expressed in second.

Galaxy – a collective term for a single system of cluster of stars, planets and other heavenly bodies residing in space in which in its center lies a gigantic black hole responsible for the effect of gravitational forces within each space bodies.

Gas – a phase of matter in which atoms are held farther apart than in solid and liquid forms.

Gravity – described as the curvature of the fabric of space. It is not merely the force pulling matter toward the center of the mass from which it resides but the entity that pushes the matter toward it.

Human – an omnivorous animal which is capable to adapt from any changes of the environment, plan ahead of the future, perceive the idea of logical reasoning, evaluate the future happenings of an event and

the leader of the food chain. Humans unlike other animals, is the sole leader of possessing higher intellectual capacity.

Hydrogen – the smallest element in nature comprising only of a single proton and neutron with one electron randomly circulating the nucleus.

Idea – any thoughts arising from your head though it could be from anything from abstract to useful thoughts that may or may not be essential to implement or applied.

Isotope – member of the family of a particular element all having the same number of protons but different numbers of neutrons.

Law of Conservation of Energy – a law stating that an energy cannot be created nor destroyed, it can only be transferred from one form to another.

Light – the ripples in space having various wavelengths distributed in all three dimensions due to any of the released energy in nature.

Light Year – the distance a specific light ray travels in a single Earth's year time. For approximation, that distance is about 9.461 trillion kilometers.

Liquid – a phase of matter in which atoms are held farther apart and loosely than that in solid but closer and more rigidly than in gases.

Magnetic Field – the resulting momentum within the material due to the collective representation of each electrons' direction of magnetic field within it.

Magnetic Field Lines – a individual line of force invisible to the naked eye emitting from the North Pole to the South Pole of a specific material.

Mathematics – a system of rule of numbers pertaining to the different areas of knowledges such as science and other mathematics related fields.

Matter – composed of particles visible or not visible to the naked human eye, which can be regarded as the occupants of space.

Milky Way – the galaxy where our solar system is located. Spiral in shape and houses various types of stars and other celestial bodies.

Molecule - a collective term for the combination of different elements in nature formed to compose various types of matter and their phases.

Neutron – a part of an atom which together with proton floats in the center; known to have neutral charge.

Nucleus – a collective name for the proton and neutron which lies on the center of every atom.

Oxygen – consists of eight protons and eight neutrons, having two electrons in its first shell and six electrons in its second shell collectively known to form a single atom.

Particle – any entity that constitutes the properties and behaviors of matter such as the acquisition of volume, its weight and mass, and other physical interactions.

Periodic Table of Elements – the table showing the list of 118 elements of nature arranged accordingly based on increasing atomic number.

Physics – the science of understanding the laws of nature from the world of quantum mechanics, in the sub-atomic realm, to the vast universes beyond the space.

Proton – a part of an atom sitting in its center together with neutron; the heaviest part within an atom.

Quantum Theory – a branch of science which deals on the study of sub-atomic particles such as electron and other particles found within the atom's structure.

Refraction – a light's property that tends to bend its pathway when moving to a denser atomic structure of water or any clear medium.

Ripples – the waves in the water or any liquid caused by the movement of any entity within it.

Shell – in atom structure, it is the region in which electrons wander around the nucleus. There are several shells within an atom and each can house different numbers of electron.

Science – a system of knowledge that deals with the study of various types of fields pertaining to the analysis and understanding of the worlds around us.

Senses – in human biology, senses are the capability of the human body to detect and measure a particular change in wavelength of light such as in vision, a change in frequency and pitch of sound, in hearing, change of chemical composition, in tasting, change in odor, in smell, and change in pressure, in feeling overall constitute to the senses that deals to perceive those traits.

Solid – a phase of matter in which atoms are held together closely forming a more tangible matter than that in liquids and in gases.

Solar System – a collective name of the planets and other bodies revolving around a star, in our case, the sun. Each planet may or may not have their moons revolving around them while rotating on their own axis.

Space – the room for mobility; any unoccupied region in which matter can move and perform mobility.

Sun – a star which lies in the center of our solar system and for clarification, not in the center of the Milky Way Galaxy. A star in which all of the eight famous planets are revolving as well as asteroids, comets and other space debris.

Technology – any means of using various types of helping devices, systems, a set of rules or a body of knowledge intended for the purpose of developing any of the human activities and goals.

Theory – a set of propositions that deals with the rules of a particular field of science and other branches of knowledge.

Time – the amount of moment an event is happening in space regardless of which observer is experiencing.

Universe – pertains to the collective term of the entirety of the space, inside and outside of our planet, beyond the stars and outside the realm of nearby galaxies, the universe is the whole spatial dimension of world we live in.

Uranium – an unstable natural element used for nuclear electric power plants together with plutonium.

Uranium-235 – the isotope of Uranium which is composing just 0.72% of the natural Uranium.

Visible Light – the range of light from 380 to 700 nanometers of wavelength responsible for human eye's vision.

Water – a kind of molecule composed of two atoms of hydrogen and one atom of oxygen held together to produce a liquid form of matter.

Wave – any existing entity that doesn't have the property of a matter such as the acquisition of volume as it existing, the attributes of mass and weight, and other physical interactions. Wave examples are light, sound, magnetism, forces and energy.

Wavelength – the overall one-dimensional length of one ripple in space composing of crests and throughs or the highest points and the lowest points of the waves respectively. Wavelength is measured either by the distance of the two crests with one through or two throughs having one crest at a time

About the Author

Austin John N. Arnaiz

Austin John N. Arnaiz is a Filipino author, writer and a book enthusiast. His passion, interest and dedication to unravel the beauty of the laws of nature in the language of Physics drove him to convert his ideas into words and craft another book for his legacy. He is the author of two books entitled; "Modern Chess Miniatures" and "What is Really Going on With That Electric Spark?" and now, his third book about the science of spaces. He is always fascinated to the fact that the universe is composed of tiny worlds and the vastness of heavenly abyss beyond human perception. It has been more than a year that the book entered its finishing touches before going to the publishing process. Now it's already finished and published. A combination of ideas and scientific information crafted in a non-fiction novel type structure altogether answering the age-old question, "Space; Is That Really Empty?" A curious question about the wonders of God's Grand Design.

Proofs that the Book is Most Likely Human Written

Dedication

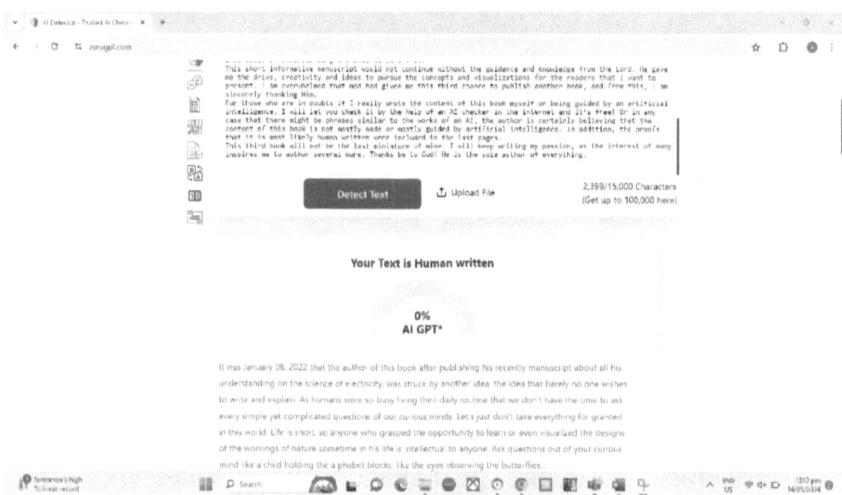

About the Book

Introduction

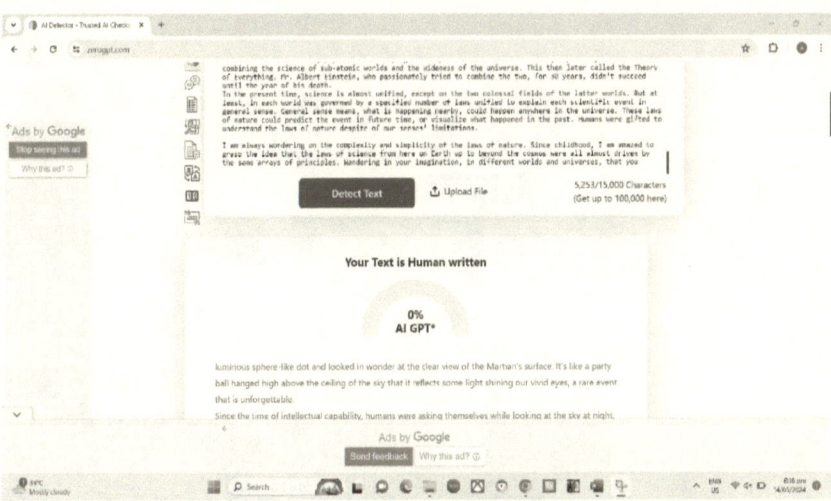

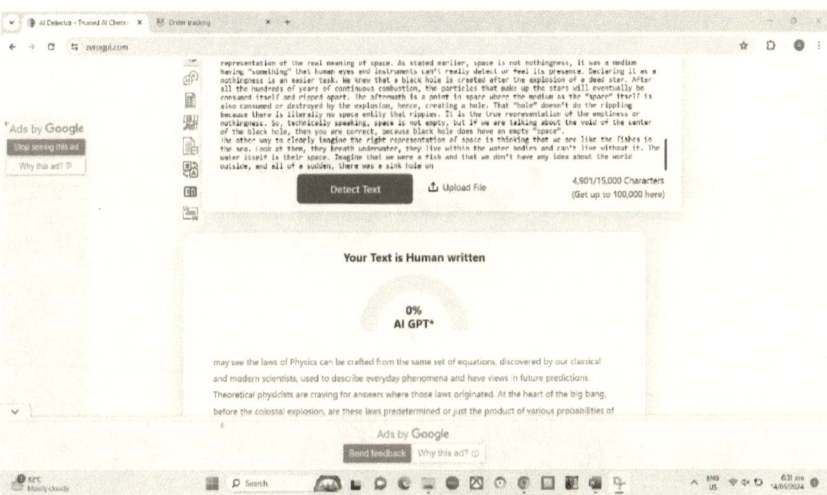

Chapter 1

Chapter 2

Chapter 3

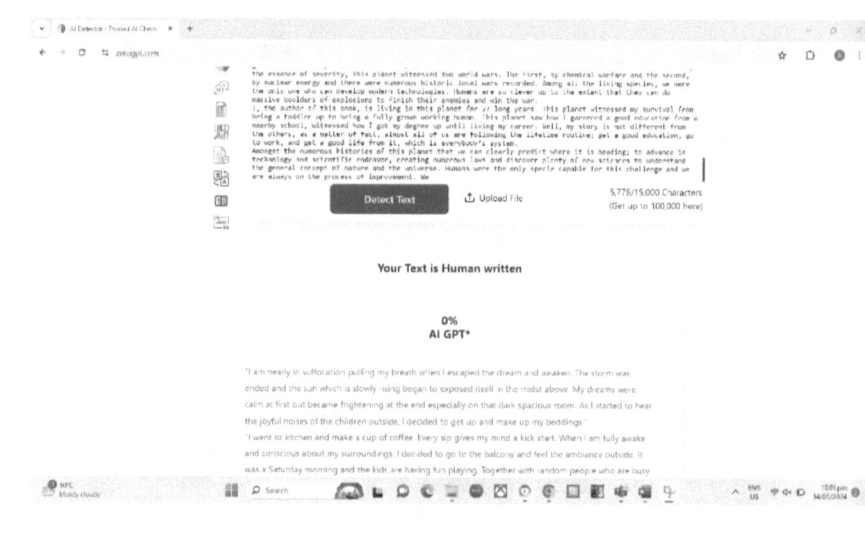

Chapter 4

68 Space: Is That Really Empty?

Chapter 5

www.ingramcontent.com/pod-product-compliance
Lightning Source LLC
LaVergne TN
LVHW041544070526
838199LV00046B/1827